Mentally Ashamed

Mentally Ashamed

By Sandra Mayfield

Sandra Mayfield Publishing

Sandra Mayfield Publishing

Clarksville Tn 37042

www.Sandramayfieldpublishing.com

phone: 931-378-1566

Published by Sandra Mayfield Publishing 09/20/2023

ISBN: 9798342286046

TABLE OF CONTENT

INTRO

I am introducing how Tennessee takes care of its supposedly mentally ill. I am writing about a place that I have visited, seen and endured. This is not about poetry it is about mental health in Tennessee.

They say Tennessee is a nice place to live, but not if you have a child or loved one with a mental condition. You don't need to move to Tennessee.

This is my first time writing about such matters, but I had to tell the public exactly what is going on in Tennessee Mental Health Hospitals.

My experience prior to me being admitted was for the lack of a better term limited by the information that I was receiving from the professionals in the field, (crisis lines, hospitals and doctors). My very first call was for one of my family members I was informed by the crisis line that you must bring them in for treatment, they stated that they couldn't do anything unless I carried them to them. If you know anything about mental illness, if you don't know any time you try to bring them in, they're not going to go with. You because they don't think anything is wrong with them. So, you must hog tie them to bring them in because they don't think that they are sick.

So, they get worse, if they stop taking their meds, think they are all right. As you would think, if you tell them they need to talk to someone they get very angry. So, you can't talk to them.

It is like trying to commit suicide to bring them in. The part that I love the most of all, in 2023, I called hotline. At first, they wouldn't tell me, that they had outpatient treatment, where they send someone to come and evaluate them and treat them if needed.

Although I have spent my entire life around mentally ill people, I had no Idea of what life had in store for me. My day started out as normal but would end with a terrifying event that changed my outlook on the world, people and what they go through.

CHAPTER 1

Dressed to Kill wrong stop

I had my day planned out. I would spend the day with a family member. We would start out by driving to Nashville headed to the IRS. I was all dressed up because I thought I was going to the IRS to clear up any messed-up paperwork. Instead, I was locked up in a mental ward. They did not ask me if it was true or not. Upon two people saying that I did something, they locked me up. So be careful of what you say to someone because anyone can have you locked up for what you did or did not say.

They carried me in an ambulance from where I was being apprehended without my consent. In an ambulance three doors down y'all, more taxpayer's money.

I was admitted July 31, 2024, without my consent. It only takes two people to tell them lies and then when they ask you if you are trying to kill yourself or somebody and you say no that should have been where they stopped and let me go. As I told them about my life story, they assumed that I was lying and made it up, so they decided to lock me in a room without any warning. I became hysterical and I asked them why they locked me in this room. They said after I had been already admitted the reason that I was there was because my husband said that I was going to cut off his privates and I was seeing things.

While I was being admitted I became hysterical. The nurse stated that she would have to call someone to put me down and I was only sitting in my seat crying. She stated that I was being hysterical, So of course, I calmed down because I was afraid for my life. She stated that if I don't calm down that she would have two men to hold me down and give me a shot. Because I was not listening to her because I was crying so hard. No sympathy for me or my situation. She just wanted to finish her paperwork and move on to her next victim.

I asked when I was going to get out and they told me that I did not legally sign myself in, so legally I couldn't sign myself. I. Ain't that a bitch?

I was in there for seven days.

More of my story at the end.

CHAPTER 2

Light Switch

This is Sandra Mayfield publishing. I'm here with a young man offering to give me his side of his stay in Clarksville, at Tennova mental health facility. What made you go to Tennova emergency room?

I was having suicidal thoughts.

Why were you having suicidal thoughts?

I had Just lost my wife.

How did they treat you when you got there?

They told them to just throw me in a holding cell.

You said it was a cell and no one spoke to you. You didn't have a room or anything?

Nope, nothing.

So, you are telling me that you told them that you were suicidal, and they took you and threw you in a cell, a small box. Wouldn't that make you think more about hurting yourself?

Yeah. without anything there to stimulate my mind, however they did, give me a book of autos. But that was like 2 days in, and I was about to leave at that point. But they just threw me in there and I didn't really. enjoy my time there and it just made me think more about it.

When was the time they let you see a doctor?

This second day.

What did Doctor diagnose you with?

Depression, I was depressed, and they were trying to send me to Nashville.

Let's see, you said the food was alright. How many times a day did they feed you?

Breakfast, lunch and dinner.

You get snacks in between?

Nope.

OK, how old are you?

27

Were you 27 when the incident happened?

Yes,

As a 27-year-old man. Thrown into a cell. You go to a hospital and. Ask for help. Did you feel like you were getting help?

Absolutely not, so just pretty much.

OK. Did they tell you anything or say anything, to you, before they did all that.

Nope. They just told me I'm going to be there for three days.

So, when you finally get there, and they throw you in a holding cell tell. Me a bit about the holding cell.

I mean the food, and everything was OK just. It was extremely silent and was driving me nuts just being there because there was nothing to do. They gave me a book to read, which I read, but other than that it's just a blank wall, and the toilets outside of the cell, pretty much so you must walk out of the cell to go to the bathroom.

You said a cell. You mean like a jail cell?

It pretty much was. It was just a small bed and a small, confined roughly closet area size with a small TV, and there's three other people in there for three days.

Did they talk to you, and let you know what's going on?

But other than that, that's pretty much what happened. Just the bathroom was always in use. So, I had the time it right to use the restroom.

This is what we endure when we are reaching out for help, and we get HELL

This is Sandra Mayfield publishing, signing off.

CHAPTER 3

In To Deep

As required and now it's recording now.

The name of this interviewee had been removed at their request

Tell me a little bit about what happened to you when you went into some of the hospitals and your diagnosis and what they helped you with and not help you with. Also, what did you think of that they could have done better?

Well, the hospitals just let you be in a room by yourself all day. They could have done a better job, they had cameras in there, but they could have checked on us more frequently in there. Other than that, they did feed us. The other one could have checked on us more frequently too. The one in middle Tennessee in Nashville could have checked on us a lot better and the food could have been a lot better. The food was nasty and seemed like cat food.

Jail when I was in there that I told them that I didn't need my medication when I first got in there. When I told them that I needed my medication they gave it to me. They were still treating me like they didn't want to give me toilet tissue, they did not want to give me shampoo or any of the other necessities. When I ran out it seemed like they were doing things for other people, other inmates, but they weren't doing things for me for some reason. You know what I mean, I don't know what they heard about me or anything like that but yeah, they did not want to give you anything. They give you supplies on the day that they were going to give you. But when you run out you run out. Don't get me wrong, they did their job for everybody else. But with me they were totally different

So, do you think that you were basically concentrating on you to make sure that your stay there was miserable?

It seemed like that yeah to get up under my skin for some reason.

What exactly where they saying when you told them that you were sick and that you needed your medicine. Did they put you in a cell by yourself?

They gave me my medicine however they did supposedly forget one night, they forgot one night supposedly. I kept on waking up throughout the night telling them that I needed my medicine that they did not give me one night. And when I told them I needed my medication they sent me to another cell, but I don't know how it is in jail or whatever, but somebody said that it was a killing cell/ pod. I was not sure why they put in there because I haven't killed nobody, so I don't know about that, but it felt like they were trying to do everything to try to get up under my skin you know what I am saying. Don't get me wrong, there were some good ones and bad ones, but they all stick together regardless.

First of all, what were you arrested for?

The thing that they came and got me for was trespassing

But how did it start the first time what happened?

Theft

Ok when you say theft what were you doing and who were you doing it for?

My kids because I was going through an episode, and you know I thought everything was on everybody else, so I started taking my kids to the store put toys the basket and tried to walk out with it

So, you were trying to make sure that your kids were taken care of for Christmas and that they treated you badly?

No, no, no it was not for Christmas they were going to play with the toys right then or when we got home

You wanted them to play with them right there in the store?

no, no, no, no we would have gone home with it then they would have played with them

I wasn't worried about Christmas. That was when I still had a job, and everything like that I didn't get fired yet or anything like that, but I did get fired eventually.

Of course, when you went down there your grandmother and your mother, and your aunt told them that you were sick and that you needed treatment. Did they send anyone there for you?

What do you mean

The emergency people that come out and evaluate you. Did they send anyone out to evaluate you?

They did I can recall because one time they did something on the screen it was Centerstone though but that was the week I was getting out of jail. But you are talking about physically come in there no they no, no. When you first go to jail, they ask you if you are on any medication and I said no. Then when I told the woman, I had been there three or four days I told them that I needed my medication. I said I had lied or what not told the police I was there a lot, so they just did there thing or what not

But the thing about it was she had my middle name as my first name and with my last name. So, I finally told them that my name was wrong. I had seen that, so I put my first name in front of it so that it read correctly. I thought it was weird and I asked her why it was listed wrong. I didn't think anything of it because I put my first name on there right away. Other than that. Then one woman came in there to evaluate me or what not, but you know I wasn't acting all crazy and stuff I was just telling them that I wanted to go. I still did not know why I was still in jail for. I should have been bonded out so or what not you know what I am saying I told them that I wanted to see my kids. I took my pill one time, but I guess that wasn't enough. She never came back after then.

The reason why you stayed longer is because they told me that they were trying to put you in the hospital. They were telling me that they were trying to assess you to see where you had to go. THEY LIED

But I wasn't acting crazy or nothing though

But still they said that they would come to you and access you

They did not do it. If that was the assessment when the woman came to the door/ cell, then yes but she just asked how you feel or what not that's it and walked off.

With your 1st stay and this stay what would be the difference in the stay and how you were treated?

You are talking about the jail or

I am talking about the hospital

They did their job it is just; they did their job it is just it was more like a jail like where someone did something bad instead of putting them in the facility instead of around real people that is where I was at the first time. Other than that, they could have had doors locked you know or what not because everybody else could come out at the same time even the criminals could come out at the same time even with the people. Even the people that weren't taking their medicine or what not stuff like that.

What do you think overall with your condition are you being helped to the best ability, or you think that they are not really feeling you or not understand you with your sickness. What were you diagnosed as?

I was diagnoses at Centerstone either bi-polar so schizophrenic one of the two or both

What haven't they still figured out?

I don't know but they have it somewhere down on paper though. I just don't remember which one it is so it could be both

Ok when you get into one of your stages as to where you feel that you can't be around anybody

I still feel like that

What do you do to control that?

I still feel that way I just tell whatever is in my head to shut up.

So, you hear voices?

It is like yeah, but I wouldn't say voices, because it be like If you believe in good and evil it is like the evil side you know what I am saying the evil side is always like negative always want to make me feel like down. I can be around people I just can't be around people a lot for a long time then it would start eating up at me. I can be around like right now it is ok you and me but if I stay here too long it is going to come out.

Do you think your medication is helping you?

To be honest yeah, I think either I was too far gone or what not. I take my medication every day and I think it is helping. They were trying to get me on the shot. I don't like the shot because I feel like if something is helping you it shouldn't hurt you. That is why I tell mama that is my belief. Because my arm hurt for four days, four days with that shot and they talk about doing it again. I don't like it.

Did they tell you what that shot consisted of?

They said that it is the liquid form of Risperdal. Because Risperdal is hard form and when you put it into your body it goes down to your liver, I am going to be honest I think there so more than that in the shot. I think they are using some type of technology or something. Some form of mind control.

Do you think you were treated better from the first time to the second time?

The first time I thought I was treated better because. I have been to three places. I have been to jail and two other places. Because I went to Tennova, Tennova was good because I was in there by myself and had a bed and a TV you know what I am saying they fed you food and not slop. Don't get me wrong in prison the jail food did get better I am not going to lie about that. Other than that jail was the worst. It is because you were in a cell and did not have TV and what not. For some reason my account did not work because I was asking my grandmother and all of them to send me money and it wasn't going to my account, and it wasn't going to my phone. They couldn't get my information because I already had my information. It was just weird because things in there don't run the same as what you are used too

With the way things are what do you think about Tennessee as far as caring for the mentally ill people?

There are no feelings involved at all, there is no sympathy so if there are no feelings or sympathy involved it is just dry it is hard. But when I was at the one in middle Tennessee, Nashville or whatever it was. I asked for the doctor and the doctor would shrug you off. I was like I am ready to go, I was taking my medication, and I am ready to go you know what I am saying. It is harder when don't have family members and you are going to be lost. They don't have to be trying to have feelings involved or understanding because they are just doing their job and have so many patients to take care of. They could have just taken 5 min out each patient a day to talk to that person. They are just going by a chart and what their employer is saying about that person. They are not going about what they see and hear. They should have let you see a doctor daily instead of every other day like Tuesday you might get out or Thursday you might get out.

But my question to you is how you feel about Tennessee and all as far as taking care of you and your sickness do you thing they are doing you right and you are getting better from it, or do you think they are half stepping and doing bare minimum, and they are not really listening to you as to whether or not you want to take a pill or shot or whatever. What do you think?

I am not going to lie they do be trying to push that shot allot, they do be trying to push that shot on people. They are not trying to force me to do the shot, but they were trying to force me. But if you are not your own man but if you are your own man, you can't let nobody do what they want to do to you. My mama, I don't know if they forced her to take the shot but if she was on the pill she may forget to take the pill, but you can always take the pill the next day. That is what I did today. I forgot to take my pill last night and just took my pill today no hurt no nothing. I was like the second time the pills hurt my back and my kidneys of what not. I would call Centerstone and leave messages after message after message and not get any calls back.

So basically, they overlooked you?

Yeah, they did.

And they did not make sure that you were alright within the system they failed you?

Yeah, I wouldn't say the system and I can't speak for everyone else's experience.

With you saying that would you please tell them how old you are?

31

So, you are 31 How long have you been having this sickness

What they told me was 3 years

Do you remember back when you were a teenager and had to go through it too?

No, I did not go through it as a teenage

You took pills when you were a teenager?

Oh yeah for my anger I didn't like the pills then. My anger got better but I still have anger issues, as you get older you learn how to control it. You don't need medication to control your anger. I didn't like the meds back then but years after that. Those meds mad men have breast. That is why I don't trust anything new. That is why I don't know why my mother took the shot. It is like Chemo. Why do you go through something that is supposed to cure you and at the same time hurts you. That don't make sense.

CHAPTER 4

Mid-Stream

They kept her in there for 13 days.

I'm here with a young lady. Miss Lady, how old are you?

I'm 30 years old.

OK, she had endured going to the hospital like I did. And she's going to tell you a little. bit of

her story. Chelsea, let me ask you a question. How was it when you first went there. Did they tell you they were going to put you there or did they put you in a cage like everybody else.

Yeah, I had no idea I was going to get put in there. I sat in the I sat at the hospital for hours and hours and hours wondering, you know, wondering what's going to happen. And finally,

After about 7 to 8 hours, they admitted me into Vanderbilt Psychiatric hospital.

When you first got there in the door in Vanderbilt Hospital, how was your treatment?

My treatment, my very first thought was, I think I'm on the wrong floor to be completely, to be completely honest, I thought I was on the wrong floor, and my next thought was how did I end up here, however. But yes, my first thought was, am I on the wrong floor and how did I get here? I wasn't expecting it to look the way that it. looked.

Explain how it looked and tell me you said you wouldn't expect it to be there. What made you look and say? I'm not supposed to be here. What was the first thing you saw to say? Hell no. I'm not supposed to be here.

Yeah. The very first thing that I saw when that said I'm not supposed to be here and no, there was a guy there and he was running around with the diaper on, and he was running around the diaper on, and he was taking off his diaper and throwing it. And they kept they the workers kept saying, you know, damn in his name. So, I said. So that's what that was. My first indication of how did I ended up on this floor or how did I end up in here?

OK, now you. Said there was like a co-ed like I had a co-ed.

Uh, yeah, it was a Co-ed. It was a Co-ed. However, the women were on one side and the men were on another.

That's what they did to me. OK. Another question, how did the staff treat you? Tell me a little bit about the staff, the staff.

Overall, I can't say the staff were helpful. Overall, I think that they could have been on their toes a little bit better the very first night when I went to sleep, I kept thinking to myself. I said, man, I just. You know, nothing happens to me just having, you know, thoughts being in a place that I'm not used to. those surroundings, the way you weren't used to those kinds of surroundings. I was not used to this type of surroundings. I opened my eyes, and my roommate was standing over me with a pillow about to smother me with her pillow, so I started screaming and then we were fighting. That's when the staff, I guess they weren't watching the cameras or whatever, you know, like they're supposed to be doing. But that's when the staff finally sat by the door. I had someone sit by the door because they didn't change my roommate. I still have the same. Crazy roommate. I don't want to say crazy. That's what I'm saying. My crazy roommate.

Hey Chelsea, they were a little bit crazy. Yeah, put it that way.

Yeah, that's what I am saying. Crazy than I was. So finally the staff started leaving our door open because we had our door cracked. They left. They just opened it completely and they sat at the end of the hall, you know, at the beginning of the door to make sure that that didn't happen.

Uh-huh.

Again, because you know, I'm. there trying to get help like everyone else. And you know, some people's conditions are going to be a lot worse than others. But I wasn't expecting, you know, to wake up with someone holding a pillow over my head.

So, It was like you feared for your life.

Yeah, it was definitely fearful. It was definitely fearful. Yes.

What did they do except by your door or whatever to make things better. Because even sitting by your door, she could have click really quick?

Yet to ensure my safety, I don't think that any other precautions. Were taken. It was just then it was just someone sitting at, you know, by the door now, because it definitely could have happened again. Thankfully, I think my mom, when she came to visit me, thankfully, she bought me a ton of shirts and a ton of different clean underwear and stuff. She's the lady. She ended up going to my things and taking a few of my clean panties and my shirt. But after she took what she needed and my mom, she bought me an excess of things, so I didn't mind sharing. But since she took them, she calmed down and she thought that we were friends after. I didn't say anything to her for taking my stuff.

Well, yeah, I had that happen to me just so they took my stuff, too. I didn't know till I got down the highway. Uh. Another question Chelsea did they tell you what kind of medication you were going to be on 1st date or what they diagnosed you with and when was the first time you had seen your doctor or your social worker?

OK. So no, I did not wait. So, when they put me when I first was in there, they did. They did tell you what their well, they give you a bunch of medicine the first night so when I told you, I didn't know what I took. I just knew I was sleeping in 5 minutes. I don't know, I don't know what it was, but it knocked me out. Eventually they did tell me what I was on because I started asking questions, they had me taking like 3 or 4 pills at one time before we got, you know, before they figure out what's exactly was wrong with you and got you on one pill, at least in my case. At Vanderbilt Hospital. I wouldn't say I met the social worker on the first day I didn't meet them, so I didn't meet my social worker until I started feeling more like me. So, she wasn't. She wasn't there before I started my medication. I didn't get to see her initially.

What you mean feel more of yourself would you explain?

Well, I, as I knew that I needed some help. I definitely knew that I needed some help, but I didn't think that I needed to be on that floor that I was on. So. So I knew that I did need some type of medicine because I could not control my mind and my thoughts. They were rampant. So, I knew that I needed some medicine, but I didn't think of the severity, and I didn't think that I needed to be on that floor. I think my condition wasn't as severe as some of the other people was in. there with me.

Yeah, that's what we are trying to get across. They put everybody in the same damn tuna can that the way I'm putting it out there, I'm letting people know that the severity they shouldn't have one set the floor for everybody else because you are scared for your life. You don't know what to expect. And everybody sleeps differently. I like. to sleep with a damn light on. So please keep the light on. But my roommate after the she's going to leave. She doesn't tell me that she liked the light off. So, I just had to concentrate and go to sleep on my own. So, what was yours?

So, I definitely like to have to sleep with the light on. That was definitely my thing. I need to see what's going on. You really could not sleep when you're there because again, you're in a place where you don't know the severity of people's conditions. You don't know and you just want to be safe at the end of the day. You want to feel safe wherever you are, right? And initially I did not. I did not feel I didn't feel safe. I had to, you know, I had to witness almost being, you know, killed with my being smothered by pillow and having my clothes taken like I was in jail.

Right. OK. Let's get back to the guy with the diaper. Why didn't they take a hand cuff him in the bed and strap him down I don't know, because that's what they're supposed to do with severity like that. and I'm sorry that you went through that. OK, that's the first time. What's the second time?

The second time I went. It was, I can say I knew what to expect the second time that I went, and it was, it was a better experience than my first. However, on my second visit, they put me on. I think it was an amazing floor. On the second visit I was put with people that were mild. Yeah, people that were going through the exact same thing that I was going through, it was parallel it was great. We had groups, we got to talk and listen to you. At least there were no men at that psychiatric hospital on the floor that I was on. Is that I went we you know we participated in different groups we had discussions we watched videos together then discussed it. It was an overall good experience overall

Different atmosphere, different, different atmosphere altogether.

Different altogether, you would have thought it was. You would have thought you. Were in a different place.

That's what they did with us, made us have groups and stuff. But what I didn't like is because they had cameras in my damn bathroom and outside the room. So, with that being said, I would like to know if something else. Your overall experience, how would you rate it because they gave you different types of medicine. You know, what the hell you were on and

somebody they're trying to kill you the first time. So, between the 1st and the second time, how would you rate Vanderbilt?

Between the 1st and the second time, I would give them a solid, a solid 5.

Thats good That's good. All right. Anything that you want to add?

I'm trying to think if the only thing I want to say is if you think you need help, definitely go out and get the help. There are places that will help you. However, read the reviews on the places if this is if this is the place that you're going. Read the reviews and read. How the staff treats you, because that's ultimately going to matter. Either you're going to be able to get the right medicine and get the treatment that you need or you're just going to go further down the rabbit hole and it's going to go on. So definitely research, research, research, whatever. If you feel that you're not feeling like yourself,

Also, another thing is they go down the rabbit hole. But when they put that guy up there and throw you up in the air. You call it, how old are you? When was the first time you needed help. How old are you now?

I was 24 years old, and I had. Had my first mental. Break.

OK, what caused your mental break?

You know what? When I went to go speak with the therapist at Centerstone in Nashville at Harriet Cohn something. I can't remember exactly. What it was called. Yeah, it might have been that. And I went there and the very first slide she put on there was most people have their first psychotic break at the age of 24 and that resonated so much with me because I was like, Oh my goodness. Like, I'm not alone. I'm 24 years old. Exactly. And here I am having my first psychotic break. So, the only thing I could think about is that I'm so happy. Uh-huh. And this sounds so childish, but I was so happy that I was still under my dad's insurance because the help that I needed at the time, the medicine that they were putting me on, I wouldn't have been able to afford that.

Bingo, Bingo. It's all about the money because a guy told me it was $53,000 just to come to his hospital. And that was in Nashville. Now we're opening the door closing with Miss Chelsea.

But I did try to escape I planned my escape route by pretending that I was sick so that they could carry me to the hospital. I made it outside with the hospital right across the street that is when I made my move I came up off the bed and started running. Keep in mind I took track and new I was in the wind and home free. When I was grabbed in midair so I guess he took track too.

This is why I called you Mid Steam you were caught in mid-stream

I would like to dedicate this to my loving mother who was there for me through all of it.

Rest in Peace Mom, I love you

Chelsea

CHAPTER 5

Got it together Depression

OK, here we go. I'm here with Felicia, Felicia White, interviewing her about her mental stage. She is going to be an addition to the book, and I want to hear her story. Felicia, what was the first thing that happened? To make you realize that you. Needed to go see someone.

Well, when I was going through it. I would stay to myself. It was a point where I didn't want to be around anybody, and I felt like at one point that everybody was against me. And I just had to realize. I was like, I don't want to keep on living. My life like. That, you know, blaming other people for my issues,

OK, you said you didn't want to be around anyone. What are you afraid of? Or were you just in a dark place where you just feel that people will hurt you if that's what it was.

I was in a dark, dark place. I'm just. I just didn't want to go anywhere, and I just didn't want to be around anybody. And I felt like I just felt hopeless in that moment.

OK. What made you seek help?

I was just tired of living the way I was living, so I just decided I would decide. For me to get up.

Did you do it on your own or does someone have to bring it to you? Or carry you. There.

No, I did it on my own. I just. I just looked up mental health and I just called the person. On my phone.

That's good. So how long have you been like this?

OH I'm 50 now so I say about over thirty years.

Over 30 years. Did they try different drugs on you, or did they just give you one and it worked.

Yeah, they tried different medications and. I've been on one medication, and it works.

What was your diagnosis?

Depression.

Did the doctor or the staff have anything to do with you? Well, did you have to go to clinics or sessions or anything like that?

I reached out to a therapist.

Are you currently seeing this therapist now?

No.

Why are you not seeing a therapist now?

Oh, because I don't know. I just, I pray, I pray and. You know, I keep myself busy. I don't think I need one.

I'm on medication, yeah.

This is my interview with Felicia White, September the 7th, 2024. My first time ever knowing that she was a depression and I've been knowing her all her little life. This is Sandra Mayfield signing out.

CHAPTER 6

Getting it back

Sandra: Today is January the 7th, 2024. I'm here interviewing KP. Who has dealt with Tennessee and Virginia, and she is going to tell us the difference between how Virginia works. With mentally ill. And how does Tennessee work? KP, so what do you think since you've been going through this all your life, right?

Most of my life I started in my 20s and now I'm 50

OK. Tell me a little bit about when you first started realizing or not realizing that. Something was wrong.

Well, I realized something was wrong. When they came to my door and were getting ready to put me in the institution in Virginia.

They weren't going to put you in an institution. I called them to evaluate you. They won't put you in an institution.

But they came to my house.

So, do you think that between Virginia, since you left from Virginia is in Virginia is getting. What kind of care were you getting in Virginia?

I was getting good care. I mean, they would listen to you. They prescribed me something that made me feel like a robot though, but they took me off that and put me on Risperdal. And when I came down here, they kept me on Risperdal.

OK. Do you see the difference? Between the how Virginia. treats the mental ill and how Tennessee treats the mentally ill. Tell me a little bit about the difference between them?

The difference is that in Virginia I was getting picked up. for my appointments, they made sure I was at my appointments all the time. They would call me. They will take care of me, when I call the case worker, the caseworker will call me. In Virginia when they take you places, they take you there and get you. back.

In Tennessee, they don't do that. In Tennessee, you must call the people. Yourself. To get you there and get. you back?

So, you have got to remember everything yourself, even though you have an illness?

Yeah, you must remember everything yourself.

OK. When you were in Virginia, when you told them you need help, did they provide help right then?

Yes, they did.

Do Tennessee do that?

No, not really. They waited until I had a breakdown in my 20s to help get me.

So Now OK, now the Risperdal you said that you are in that now, OK, do you take the orally or injections?

I take both oral and injections. I don't take it anymore though. I don't take Risperdal no more.

OK. Why?

Because I'm on naveta it is a different type of schizophrenic pill. I take the

shot and the pill at the same time. The pill makes me go to sleep. The shot makes me go, day-to-day.

OK, what's the difference between what you were diagnosed with at first and what you're diagnosed with now?

They said I was bipolar. And then they said I was schizophrenic, paranoid schizophrenic. So, when I was diagnosed bipolar, I was up in Virginia. When I came down here, I was diagnosed with schizophrenia, paranoid schizophrenic.

Do you remember any things that you do while you're under that. And not on your meds?

Yes, I remember most of it. I really do. I hate that because I put my kids through a lot.

OK, tell me a little bit about that?

Well, I lock them outside the door. I had my daughter run around with me. So, I thought I was pregnant and all this other stuff and just I put them through a lot.

OK. But you were sick. OK, why did you stop taking your pill?

They stopped. Giving it to me because the insurance wouldn't pay. Well, when I was in my 20s and 30s the insurance wouldn't pay for my brain tumor pill and the Risperdal itself. They wouldn't pay for both,

So, it's all about Tennessee and insurance.

Yeah. So, I couldn't have one or the other. I had to get. I had to skip a month. Every time then when I stopped taking my pills, the doctor told me that he wasn't going to give it to me. I need to go to Centerstone and get my pills.

Why is that?

I don't know.

What doctor did that say on record?

I forgot his name.

What? What clinic was he working out of?

Matthew Walker. The one on Dover Road He's working at that clinic at Matthew Walker

Was that the only clinic you can go to at the time?

No, that wasn't the only clinic. But he told me to go to Centerstone because they might have to adjust my medication.

OK, when you decide to go to. Centerstone. That's thoroughly, but he was. So do you. Do you hold the doctor responsible for that?

Yes, I do. Because he really gave me the medicine and I could have gone ahead and gone to Centerstone if you would give me the medicine, I would have a straight mind to go to, Centerstone. He stopped giving me my medication altogether. He wouldn't give it to me for like a whole month.

Have you asked him why he did that?

No, I never asked but he did stop working at Mathew walker and started working for Centerstone. But I think they got rid of him at Centerstone because I haven't seen him there either.

So, do you think the state of Tennessee took care of you?

No, no, they don't. They don't take care of their people. No, they don't.

OK. With your illness now, do you have to pay for any of your meds?

I have to pay a copay.

OK. KP, how do you feel that you are, as of today, January the 7th, 2024?

I feel happy now. I'm happy that I'm on my medication. I'm happy that I know that I can go to Centerstone anytime I want, and you know, any day I want. I got a great doctor.

What's that doctor's name?

Dr. CS.

CS, how long you been treated by her?

OH. It's been years. It's been years.

OK, so right now you are content with what you have at Centerstone?

yes. I have a doctor. I have a case worker. I have a nurse, and I had a therapist. But I let go of that therapist because I didn't need it anymore. I didn't need them anymore.

OK. So, you feel right now that you are right? What's the pros and cons?

The pros I know, they know pros and cons, but what is the difference between being diagnosed bipolar and being diagnosed? Schizophrenia and they come hand in hand.

Yes, it does. Yes, it does.

OK. But with Bipolar it's your mood swings. Yeah, but something that's not the thing is your bipolar the way your bipolar work, it's two different kinds of mental illness. You know that, right? OK. So, what is one stage?

Yeah. Yeah.

You were diagnosed with bipolar. What made them turn over and say you was diagnosed with schizophrenia?

Because I was seeing things, I was hearing things. I was believing things I couldn't recognize my kids. I couldn't recognize my momma. I couldn't recognize my kids; I couldn't recognize my kids at all. And my mom at all. I couldn't recognize you guys at all. The only person I could recognize is my sister, and I thought she was coming by to, you know, get me.

Uh-huh. So, you thought your sister was there for you to help you to come. and get you. When you found out your sister won't come and get you, how'd you feel?

I don't know. I don't know. I guess I went back to sleep because I was in bed.

So OK, that's it for KP. My name is Sandra Mayfield. I'm doing a book on the schizophrenia, the mental ill, the bipolar, and other illness like Autism which sometimes gets diagnosed. Because the symptoms are so similar.

CHAPTER 7

Almost deadly fall

Hello, this is Sandra Mayfield publishing. I'm here with a young man to have something to say. About his stay. When he was in the hospital again, Tennessee. So, what exactly was your first impression the first day you were there? Kentucky vs Tennova?

Tennova it's so icky there. They almost kind of let me die when I tried to end my life, they didn't do anything. I had to make myself throw up. But the mental hospital, it was all right. It wasn't in Tennessee. It was all the way in Hopkinsville.

Sandra So Kentucky is better than Tennessee, when it comes to mental health.

Yeah.

 What? What? Tell me something about your little. Stay in Kentucky. Here we go, Tennessee.

Well, the Kentucky stay, it was anything crazy. It wasn't like, you know. Whoa. Something raves about. It was. I feel like it was just a normal mental hospital. How it should run with nurses that care for you and watch out for you and stuff like that.

See, I'm not just making this up y'all Tennessee. Again, this is Sandra Mayfair. Do you have anything else you want to add to this.

No.

Your dinner and all that there. How did they feed you?

It was bland, but it was filled with protein. I would say we always had a lot.

Did they have anything for y'all to do.

Yeah, we had a gym where I worked out and played. Basketball a lot.

I have never heard that. Can I say come on now? This is Sandra Mayfield signing off. Thank you.

CHAPTER 8

The Light Bulb Off

And I have a young man, and I'm doing the interview. Uh, hello. how are you baby? How old are you? He's 27 years old and he has been in and out of hospitals, so I'll let him tell his story again. He's 27. And here's his story. OK, when was the first time you knew that you had to be admitted? And what did you think when you first arrived at the mental institution.

27.

Right there.

Well, it wasn't my choice by being admitted, I kind of have bipolar phases and I try to hurt myself many times.

OK, so did you have? When was the first episode your very first episode?

Let's see. I think that was around 2019.

This is 2024 now. So 2019, OK. And when you were there, how was your care? How did they treat you when you first walked in, what did you expect and what did you see?

I'm well. Clearly, I wasn't feeling at home. I mean, like they were kind of tough on us.

Hold on, tough?

Hold on for a second? Tough. What do you mean, tough?

Just by how they would say things make us do different things by, you know, having those basically go outside. We had to do some cleaning up as well.

Like what? So, in other words. They have free labor, yes. OK, continue.

Yeah. Yeah, it wasn't anything extensive, though. They gave us our medication and they gave us 3 meals a day.

OK.

But you know, it wasn't really good food, clearly.

Yeah. OK. What some of the bizarre stuff that you have seen. Did you see anything that you knew that you weren't supposed to be on that level?

Not that I know of.

OK, so All in all, what was your treatment? How many facilities have you been to?

Well, I've only been to one that I know of, but I've been there 13 times.

You didn't know about the 13 times. What's that?

Why have I been 13 times?

Now, why you didn't know that you've been there 13 times. What they gave you over, medicate you or what? I'm just asking the questions as to why you were there 13 times and don't remember.

OH, I remember being there just about all the time. But some of them not, but that's because of my seizures. And you know, I did have. I did do a lot of drugs and alcohol back then too.

 OK.

Yeah, but it was mainly because of the seizures that I was having. I think the seizures also have something to do with the bipolar disorder that I have as well.

OK. Well, you know there's different types of bipolar because they said I'm bipolar. So, with that being said, what was the harshest thing that you think that they can change or do better at Tennessee hospitals?

What do I think they could? Can do better.

Yes.

Well, to start off with, I think they would be able to, you know, treat their patients a little bit kinder. I mean like the patients are going through so many different things and a lot of them don't even know how to handle themselves. And that's what the nurses and doctors are supposed to be there for. So, I think. You know, they could be. A little bit more compassionate to their patients.

Bingo. That's exactly what I said. When was the first time you seen your doctor? What date? How many days were you there before you seen your doctor?

I don't know because I don't have a particular doctor. I haven't had insurance since I was a little boy. So, I always must see somebody new and different.

Each and every time. OK, so do you feel like you were mistreated? Because being a human, and they think that you're not. I'm not going to add any words cause if I add words and they think I'm coaching you. But do you think that they were doing y'all like that because they thought that y'all didn't have the right mind or Y'all were just inhumane?

OH, I mean like that's a tough one, but. I mean like I kind of do think in a way that it was because we were out of our right mind, you know, so they were kind of taking advantage of it in some ways by, you know, making us do some work and everything too.

Mm-hmm.

But yeah, I could also say that it was inhumane in some respects and like, you know, we weren't able to go outside or anything. You know, we could only stay on the TV for So long and.

MHM. Did you have a social worker?

I did not.

Oh wow. So, all that time he was there and the time in between, you never had a social worker. Tennessee I always put at the end of everything I say because I want everybody to know that Tennessee is not right. All right, young man, I'll thank you for this interview and you have a nice one. Bye.

Conclusion

Don't throw me away!

Is this Sandra Mayfield I am talking about nursing homes and homes where you send our loved ones when they get older, or they get a something like a disease that you can't take care of. Now I'm not. An expert on this, but I do know how people feel when they leave their home. You see, my mother got sick, and they kept telling me to put her in a home. My mother said she wanted to pass in her own home. So, when you put someone in those kinds of places, it's just like put them in the mental ward. They half take care of them. They wind up with bad sores. They wind up not eating, be forced to eat where they tie them down, put them down and forced the food down them. Also, they stay and their soiled clothes for a while, just like they do in the. mental ward. You look up and you, think that your loved one is. being well taken care of. No, they're not. You know, and you have some people that. You look up, you have some of them that. When you take, their freedom or that home atmosphere away from them, they deteriorate faster. So, if you have someone that you love dearly and you feel that you can't take care of them. Let them do in their own home. Try to find some kind of way to do for them in their own home. Please take care of them at home because they brought you in this world. Don't discard them because they elderly or whatever. I'm 70 years old myself, so with that being said, I think that what have I? I have observed that people function better when they in their own surroundings. Now, I'm not talking about the ones that have. Oh yes. I am because regardless of where they can remember or can't remember they still, want to be in their home. Were. they have been all their lives. You take them out of the atmosphere, their surroundings, they do not get well, they're depressed. They don't have no one there to love. So, if you love them. Take care of them the right way.

When you're mentally ill, you don't want to tell anybody because of the stigmatism behind it. They think you're crazy and you don't know what you're talking about. They don't want to be your friend because you might breathe on them, and they catch what you have. It is a lot to that stigmatization, that's why I name the book Mentally Ashamed because you, too, embarrassed to tell anyone about their staying in the hospital or about you being on medication for your mental illness? They call you medication crazy pill. What people don't know is that you are not crazy. It's just that some of us have a chemical imbalance. But mine came from the lack of rest, and stress. A lot of things can trigger a person's mental state. Some of our solders, both men and women come back from the war, you know, they have PTSD and so on and therefore, are they crazy, would you say that? What category would you put them in? They have feelings but have experienced something very traumatic when someone experienced a traumatic experience like I experienced a whole lot of traumatic experience, but I am not mentally ill. It's just the way I think. And the way I do things is different. What you might do and what exactly do you consider crazy? Is it crazy when someone get out there and rape a 1000 women and men? Would you consider them as crazy or someone get up and mistreat children, rape them and beat them and kill them? Would you call them crazy? Are they supposed to be in the mental institution too?

When I was up there, they kept saying I got to touch them like there's some kind of flesh-eating disease that can rub off on them or some kind of insect. That's what I'm talking about. They don't even want to touch you because they think that they don't want to catch what you have, but you do not have anything. I the only thing it would take is a warm heart, a true heart. And a hug to let them know they are human because they are instead of treating them like some disgusted animal you just picked up outside and was wounded. And you want to see if you can bring it back, but you don't want to. Really touch it.

Before I forget this one, I remember one night, they turned around and was looking for us. I forgot what it was for. I don't think it was at night it was in the morning, I guess, to take the temperature or something. But anyway, the remark was, they just like cockroaches, you know? Whenever you turn on the light cockroach run, that's what she said. We were just like cockroaches so not only do the treat you bad they talk about you too. And the people that work in this industry they don't give a damn about you, period. Only thing they think about is when they're going to get paid. And how fast they can go home!

I was just thinking I got a bill today from. My insurance company, guess what? They put me down as having. gastric problems. They did not bill the insurance company to say they set me on the damn mental ward because they knew I was not supposed to be there. In the first place the man behind that booth, acted like he was God. like in the airplane booth for something that one had his hand up. Yes, I know to put me in there. So, whoever he is, someone please get hold to him and I'm going to name the hospital so y'all can't get him. Because he stood behind that booth and decide whether you're going in or out. But you made the wrong decision when it came to me. Now I'm thankful in a way that he did that because, I got to see and go through those things firsthand instead of just what I guess or what someone told me. So. I am trying my best to get all this out of me cause it's still bothering me right now. I mean I'm still not fully heal from that. I mean I'm still emotional damaged behind that because it took a lot out of me. I'm scared about my freedom. I mean, if someone can lock, lock you up just because someone said that you said you was going to do something to them. So, like everybody would be locked up, don't you say? So, with that being said. With society and the way, we're supposed to be one person or two, people shouldn't be able to, like I say one, because that man behind that glasses who told them to take me in there because I wouldn't bowed down to him. And I'm not going to ever bow down to anyone.

Even if I am wrong, I admit that I am wrong, but I am not going to bowed down to you because you are not more superior than I am. You know we all have a thing on this earth that we are put here to do, and mine is to tell the truth and let people be aware of what's going on around them. I am going to talk a little bit about your significant other, parents and people in the insane asylum or a nursing home it's not good. Because they lose that intimate touch from their loved ones.

Those employees are there just for a paycheck and. they don't give a damn about you and your loved ones. You know! So that is why I want everybody to know right now to be very thoughtful as to how put someone somewhere that they don't have control of you know. Just like when they put those children in prison and stuff, they wind up dead or something, you know you wind up dead you can't go nowhere, and they gone tell me since I didn't bring myself in there, I can't release myself. I said hold up I said that I was going to take treatment even though there was nothing wrong that I could see. So again, be very grateful for the freedom that you have because it can be taken away from you in a lackaday split.

There were interesting people that I met while I was in there one of them, I am not releasing her name. She had been in a mental hospital in West Tennessee where you would have to fight for your life daily because of poor staffing and not having enough people to handle the volume of patients so they had to fend for themselves.

The four Amigos kept me going and to realize who I am and not what they want me to be. We are all a little crazy in our own way but there is no reason to be locked up in a mental institute, Is it?

The four amigos as I like to call them. Every night they give the staff hell. One would go one way, the other go the other way. And they do something to make the staff run around in circles. The nights when they do that it was very enjoyable because you see how people mind work. To the staff, they might be sick and untouchable, but they had them going. They were smarter than the staff. So, you think about it just cause one part of the mind isn't working another part is. To outsmart the staff, that have a college degree. Come on. Now. You know what I'm talking. About its. Really funny if you were there, you would be laughing too. And I'm still laughing. Because they gave me some joy at the end of the night, I knew I had something that was going make me laugh.

We should ask ourselves how do you classify people that will prey on innocent children and on the elderly. What are they? Mentally ill. No, they're not. They're just greed and nasty. They want self-gratification, so they prey on children, pray on elderly, so how do you define them? You can't, but you define bipolar, schizophrenic. You defined the other one. That. No one wants to speak of, and that is when a child commits suicide. You called them crazy or just out of control. Which do you call them? Because they've been neglected or mistreated, and they feel the world don't have anything else to offer them. So how do you categorize them? You call them crazy. we call them crazy because they've been through a lot, and they need something to calm their brain. How do you define them? How do you classify them?

What do you call them are you scared to be around them. You don't know. You don't know, you don't know who is crazy and how to specify crazy, but you will call them crazy. Because they're not. So how do you categorize crazy or someone's steeling your money? Or someone betraying you are they crazy? No. So define crazy for me.

Tell me?

When all is said. In the end. It was a scary place. An unforgettable stay. And I never want.to go there again so.